Close The Door Before The Night Comes In

By

Linda L. Bielowski, PhD

Dedication

To My Beloved

Author of Life / Death…Time / Space

Alhamdulillah!

Preface

All my former poetry books began with lengthy introductions, but this one will take a different path. This is an array of meditative pieces evincing the spiritual struggle~~the tug-of-war~~intrinsic to our flesh/ soul; dust/divine ephemeral selves. They confront the perplexity of our birthright…our perceived separateness from whence we came and our intense craving for reunification with our Source. So I raise my bread bowl filled with poems to the reader… my companion seeker and sojourner: *Savor!*

~~Linda L. Bielowski, PhD~~

Contents

Close The Door Before The Night Comes In

Close the door before the night comes in
Creeping about like a deceiver in our bedroom
Tarnishing wedding bands and tearing at vows till gold turns to rust
A mad mongrel tugging the cover let's with his rotten teeth

Close the door before the night comes in
Varnishing the floorboards with sticky tar
Besmearing the walls with flaky smut
A doomsayer foreshadowing demise

Close the door before the night comes in
But fear not, forget not
Looking through the bare window
How bright the light shines in darkness

Whirling Dervish

In the dungeon
During a dark night of the soul
Dance…
For you, my friend, are the light…the soothing light
A cool compress on the forehead
A flicker of the Beloved
Within the searing wound of ego doubt and despair
Dance…

Dry Season

In a dry season
The splintered raft sits on bedrock
It's face a relief map of veined rivulets turned to talc
Where is the stream of Believing
Where is the dear Beloved
Amidst this millstone of nothingness and dread
If the *One* I seek is seeking *Me*
Truly…truly
Give me fresh sight to find water
In a dry season of doubt

Poor In Spirit

I am a stone
The echo in a hollow cave
Poor in spirit
Caressing my idols
I count my coins and hoard my corn
Deaf to the sparrow's song
Blind to the holy dawn
I stumble on my prayer rug woven with braided pride

Leaven

Looking outward
Why do you search the surface
Sifting the soil
Picking at crumbs
When you are the leaven
Looking inward
You possess the whole loaf
The bread of life breathing within the soul

One

Peering through smoke and mirrors to glimpse Paradise
Beyond the grasp of sin and shame
Untethered
Free to be
A blade of grass
A green bud
ONE…
In love unfettered

Will You...

Will you walk to a mystical cove
Dance around rock walls
Fall face down to meet the earth's caress
Beyond the ego corral and the pride pen
So hard…So easy to journey there
The blueprint is etched in your marrow
As familiar as a Beloved's kiss

Shooting Crows

The man who shoots crows
Stands on a lush hillock
Polished rifle pointed at heaven
Shots pierce the silent farmlands
One! Two! Three!
Black feathered bodies hit the ground like fallen angels
Shaking his fist at God
For the son carried afar in a doll casket
Buried in ancestral clay before his time
Sweet baby's breath turned to sour milk
A mother's breast dried up by mourning
The hunter stunted by loss in a long, bleak winter of the heart

Red Tide Coming

It's the season of algae blooms
Red tide raging in
A blood sacrifice of sea creatures and shellfish
The beach becoming a cemetery of shallow graves
Beside the carmine and cinnabar tainted waters

It's the time of spirit storms
Red tide tumbling over
A bloodletting of belief and balance
The soul becoming a barren place of bewailing woes
Beneath the crimson and cardinal tinged wounds

Shhh…
Red tide coming

Call To Worship

Bunny in the brushwood
Ears straight as oars in the water
She knows and hears the *Voice*
Moving through her insides like rolling thunder and raw wind
Not a nose quiver…stilled
Obeying *His* captivating call to worship

Trusts

The branch stripped of bark
Sinews of wood, thin and stretched like spaghetti, touch the trunk
table
Trusts…

Bent over the frosty river
Hung between air and water like a feather
Trusts…

An imagination feeling wings spread horizon wide
Gliding like a hawk
Trusts…

Alive in the given moment
Surrendered to the future unseen
Trusts…

One God
Lord of the Universe
Creator of all
All compassionate, All merciful
Have mercy on me

Make me a willow instead of an oak
That I might bend and bow like a ballerina
Nose kissing the hard ground
I am the broken branch who
Trusts…

Blind Beggar

Raise your begging bowl high at twilight
Like Oliver Twist hungry for porridge
Looking for scraps from the Last Supper
Ready to settle for morsels
When freely given a moveable feast
A picnic spread on the spacious lawn
Your portion prepared with limitless love
How blind the beggar who spits at faith

Winter Feast

Outside the bay window curtained in lacy light of filigree
Snow flaked birds soar and sweep for bits of corn
Like persistent miners panning for gold
Captives in a winter feast to feed the grateful core

Waxy-Walled Separation

How do I pray?
Eyes closed, head bowed, hands folded

In a wee child's whisper with the words from a favorite bedtime prayer
Or an anguished plea with the beating of fists against my breast
Perhaps in Hillsong with the shooting of a solar flare
Or feral dancing under liquid lunar light
Reclined in a hammock with the swaying from a phantom breeze
Supine on round earth with gazing into star-sapphire sky
Kneading dough with fingers drowning in the sticky depths

I pray without praying…passing through
In the melting away of waxy-walled separation

Words Cannot

Words cannot contain you
How do you capture the essence of *One* who is *ESSENCE*
Names for you taste like cardboard and leave me longing
So far from you…waving farewell…moving farther and farther
from shore
A distant spot of spirit and flesh
Waves of confusion roll and tumble me
I cannot find you…I cannot call out to you
Because…how should I address you
Allah, G_d, Vishnu, Father, Beloved…on and on
Sit…stand…kneel…touch my nose to the earth…whirl and
dance madly
Words cannot contain you…cannot touch you
I just want to feel you like a wet, cool cloth on my hot head
Soothing…soothing the ache too deep to finger

Unselfing

My Beloved, One Deity
Master of the worlds, Maker of eternity
Unconditionally compassionate, Unceasingly merciful
Do you have a preferred name…a particular path to your
feet…to the door of your heart
I have sat beside sheiks, shamans, sages of every dominion
Poured over their holy books and memorized their scripts until my
mind screams with confusion and conflict
Questions…searching…questions…few answers
I am an open sore who seeps and weeps with sadness waiting
for you
What of the loyal one whose lips shape every name
Whose knees rub the soil in a thousand reverent ways…whose
soul yearns for *unselfing*
Like brave snow melting…letting go of form and boundary to join
the universe in a drop of morning dew

My Eternal Playwright

I will meet you somewhere, sometime, my Beloved
But why *someday*—
When the magical dust of creation fills bone and flows blood in
me now
Your breath in my nostrils like wind in the meadow
When you seal sweet morning with a secret kiss
My fluttering eyelids adjusting to a fresh day
On the open curtained stage we share
You the author of time
My eternal playwright

War Paint

*For Barb

I knew a woman who would go womb wild
During a bipolar phase under the full moon
She would put on her thick war paint and ceremonial dress
Off she would go to shop for young warriors at the Greyhound
She would take them to her single room to play with like tin soldiers
After a day or two the greasy war paint would smear and smudge
Sage and sweet grass turning to sweat and tears of regret
Then the woman would repent for her sins
Searching for a savior between the lines of her poetry
Writing alone in her private place
Plain faced and covered on the downside under a slip of moon

Found

Mom,
You slipped through the thin spaces
Like a mosquito through a screen in June
Lifting the veil to full vision
Face to face with the Beloved
And I questioned why you couldn't come back to this foggy feeble side
Unable to fully grasp or accept where you'd gone
This puzzling passage

Mom,
Wish you could tell me how to find the Divine
I've read chapter by chapter, verse by verse, in the holy books
Immersing myself in them till my eyes grow dim, my head heavy
Each wisdom writer offering barely a glimpse of Whom I desire
Then I opened the silver locket round my neck
Looked into your gleaming face and felt the One God holding my heart
Rocking it gently in an otherworldly Moses basket

Safe—
Found

Drink From The River

Grandpa,
I drink from our river
Beside timid white-tail deer and furtive coyote
Hawks do their glorifying circle dance, eyes darting
While doves gather on the ground
A choir in their wings, a calm in their coos
Common starlings aligned on the wooden gate like deacons in
glossy black suits
Sunflower seed cake and suet for tithing
Lone garter snake basking in a sunny corner next to my chimney,
certain he doesn't belong
An abandoned hen house sits near a lookout point
Feral cats squat there in the cold
They come to me like children to Jesus
It took me half a lifetime to return here
Year after year, dreams of sleepwalking among the familiar
Only to awaken in disbelief, disappointment, and despair
But a year ago I landed here in a snowstorm
A lost catboat reaching port
I saw a man with low flat cap who resembled you in profile,
pausing at the front of my driveway
Then you slipped away into shadow space to drink from the Jordan
We drink from the river, *Grandpa—You and me...*

Let The Night Come

Open the window and let the night sweep in
Settling around your shoulders like a prayer shawl
Whispering like a lover framed in perfect memory
Nothing to fear
Not for but friend
Unlatch the lock
Let the night come